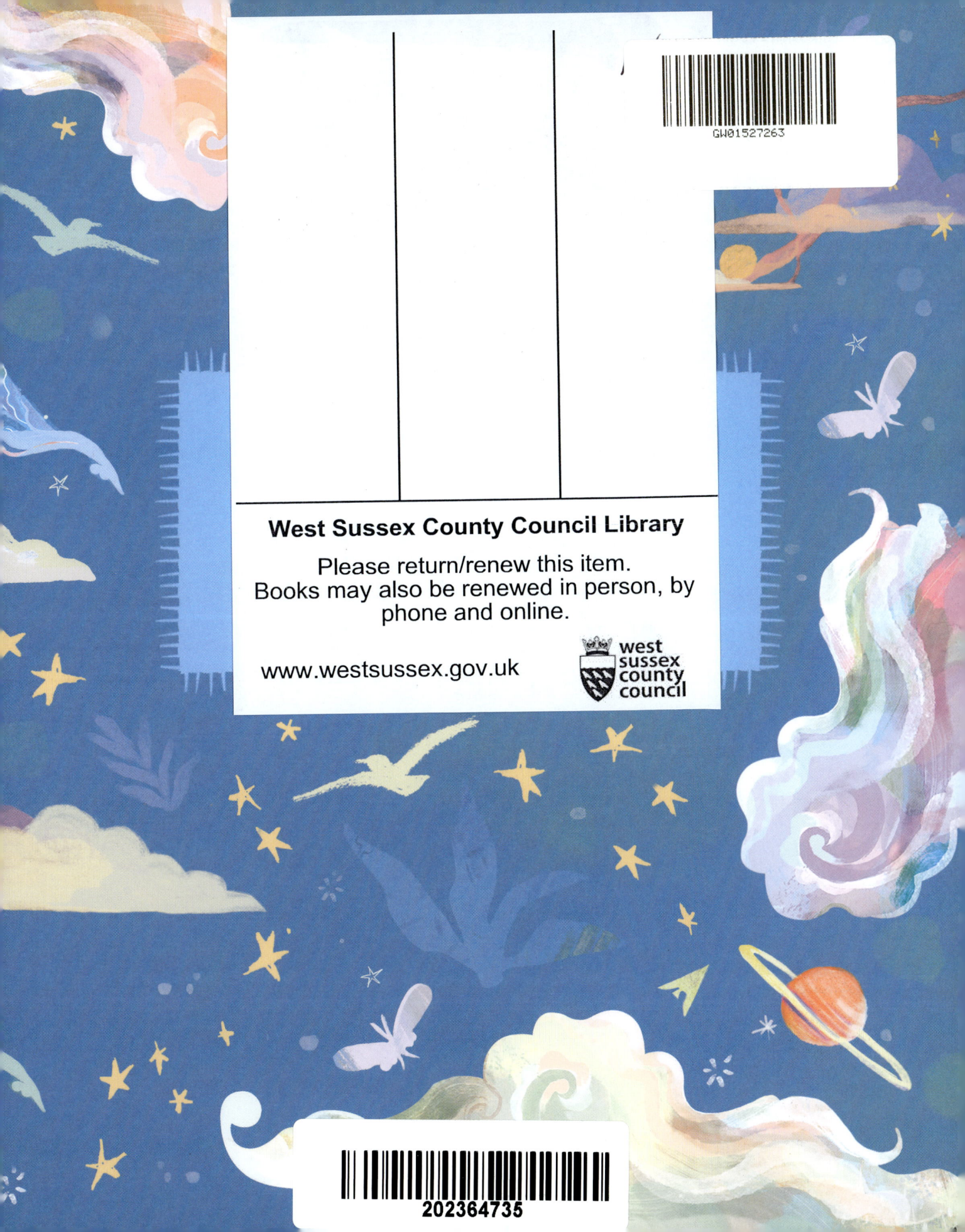

Introduction

In poetry there is a kind of quiet magic. For all its wordy wonder, it holds a hush at its centre – a silence that promises refuge from the hustle and bustle of the world while giving us the space to hear and understand its noise.

This balancing act is similar to the practice of mindfulness: the art of paying attention to yourself and the world without judgement. Both teach us to marvel at the present but also to recognise how small and fleeting every moment is. From exploring our own thoughts and feelings to learning to admire the tiniest details of our surroundings, the works in this anthology demonstrate how mindfulness and poetry can help us slip out of the everyday and see things anew.

And with this deeper understanding of the world comes a deeper understanding of ourselves. What could be more magical than that? Like a spell, poetry wields the right words at the right time and has the power to transform us.

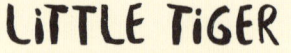

LITTLE TIGER
LONDON

Contents

6   You Are Here – *Mandy Coe*

8   I Wished into a Wishing Well – *Jack Prelutsky*

10   My Rock – *Pat Mora*

12   The Ink Cure – *Kate Wakeling*

14   How Easily – *James Carter*

16   Your Dream Is – *Jason Reynolds*

18   A Lesson from the Trees – *Nikita Gill*

20   Listening for Silence – *Joseph Coelho*

22   The Colours of My Dreams – *Valerie Bloom*

24   Soft Like Bed Sheets – *Amina Jama*

26   The Rhythm of Life – *Michael Rosen*

28   Taking Care of Small Things – *Sue Hardy-Dawson*

30   The Tree That Time Built – *Mary Ann Hoberman*

31   My Inner Weather Report – *Georgia Heard*

32   Pausing Phases – *Sophia Thakur*

34   Anger's Secrets – *Sanah Ahsan*

35   From *Clap When You Land* – *Elizabeth Acevedo*

36   The Magic Box – *Kit Wright*

38   Over the Weather – *Naomi Shihab Nye*

40   Hide and Seek – *Zaro Weil*

42   Biographies

45   Copyright and Acknowledgements

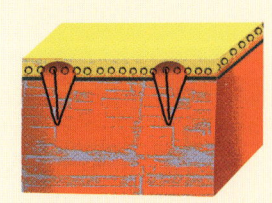

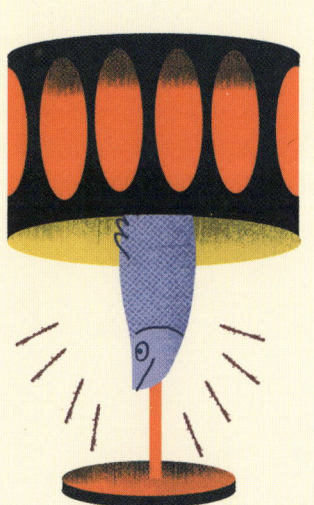

You Are Here

In the car park is a map of your town.
Everyone presses their finger
on the red dot that says,
You are here.

And here you are!
Inside your shoes, inside your skin
and beneath your hair,
on freshly cut grass, a double-decker bus,
or in bed, slipping into a dream.

In a map of your day
you are here, bookmarking
this page, passing ginger biscuits,
dodging umbrellas
as you dash through the rain.

You are blowing on a hot chip
and laughing with a friend.
Breathe in the smell of vinegar
and place your finger on this moment.

You are here! You are here!

Mandy Coe

I Wished into a Wishing Well

I wished into a wishing well,
my wishes were in vain.
I tried to catch a rainbow,
but it vanished like the rain.
I dug for buried treasure
till my shovel came apart.
I heard a rhyme inside my head,
and now it's in my heart.

Jack Prelutsky

My Rock

    Summer's ending.

I sit on my desert rock, listen
        to the world's hum.
            Crows and ravens caw,
finches and sparrows chirp. A dog barks.

    Can I face
        the halls of judgments?

A breeze strokes my face,
      brings me back to spiders
and lizards busy at their chores,
      private conversations—
sights and sounds I savor.
      This earth, my home.

High on the vast blue canvas,
        clouds curl, float.

Taking a deep breath, I gather myself.
    I bring what I am.

Pat Mora

The Ink Cure

When I'm feeling sad
or stuck
or flat
or when my brain
is knotted up
with worried thoughts
of this
and that,

I've found a thing
that often sets me right
and shifts my mood
from dark to light.

I fetch a pen and paper
(any sort will do)
then settle at a tabletop
or bus stop bench
or patch of floor
(you do not need a pretty view)

and then I tell this hand of mine
that grips the pen:
now go explore.

I don't mind what it writes
or draws.

It might be words
or squiggly lines
or a doodle of ten tiny birds flying through an open door.

The only rule is not to stop
and not to think.

Just let the ink
fill up the page
from base to top
or round and round
or side to side.

Let the pen
be your guide.

Let those troubles go.

And as the ink finds its way,
you too may find
some bright new
thoughts
begin to
grow.

Kate Wakeling

How Easily

the present
escapes into the past.
Like raindrops on a lake,

like moths into the dark.
That afternoon you learnt
to swim. The night

you tried to count
the stars. Ever passing
through your hands,

moments disappear
like sand. So catch them.
Trap them. Write them

down. Preserve them
as your memories.
Turn them into

words

      like

            these.

James Carter

Your Dream Is

Your dream is the mole
behind your ear,
that chip in your
front tooth,
your freckles.

It's the thing that makes
you special,
but not the thing that makes
you great.

The courage in trying,
the passion in living,
and the acknowledgement
and appreciation of
the beauty happening around
you does that.

Jason Reynolds

A Lesson from the Trees

When the world feels like
more wound than world,
and worry has curled
like ivy around your mind,
look to your window
for the trees are inviting you outside.

They have been there longer
than you and me,
tall and grand and ancient as can be
through wind or hail or stormiest of skies,
they stand strong as their leaves
wave and dance and fly.

And if your mind is still in fearful tatters,
to the trees that will not matter,
for they have been there for a hundred years
listening to the fears and joys of a thousand birds,
and with the same grace and kindness,

they will listen to you too,
and show you that the answer
to all of life's storms
is to be patient
and stand strong.

Nikita Gill

Listening for Silence

It's like threading a needle,
holding marbles in oiled hands,
honey-hive diving with a stick
or making out the shape of your bedposts
in your ink-black room.

      Listening for silence.

I would seek it out
between the page turns of library books,
find it stuffed in the corners of packed lifts,
listen to its emptiness –
      too brief, too rare.

I travelled for more:
sought its closemouthed delight
in Mexican caves.
    But the bats would chitter.
Dove deep for its clammed-up splendour
in the Dead Sea.
    But the bubbles would plink.
Climbed through the clouds for its wordlessness
in a non-vocal balloon.
    But the winds would whisper.

The silence was gone – impossible to find.

Tongue-tied,
I zipped my way home,
hungry for hushed notes,
desperate for muted tones.
Saddened.

In the espresso of my night room
I closed my eyes and listened.
Outside – cars, sirens, winds.
Inside – the creaking house, my breath, my heart.
But, under it all, for the first time I notice –
silence.

Silence – not hidden among the noise.
No.
Silence – the silk from which noise is ruched.
The mother of noise.

Pushing the winds, carving the sirens,
holding the rumble of the cars... silence.

Moulding the creaks of my house – silence.
Bellowing my breath – silence.
Hugging the beats of my heart – silence

Joseph Coelho

The Colours of My Dreams

Once I held inside my palms
the curviness of a bow,
and listened in the cornfield
to the sadness of a scarecrow.

I clearly saw the saltiness
of the Atlantic Ocean,
watched a mother with her newborn babe
and tasted her devotion.

Once I heard the vibrant green
of a lawn that was just laid,
smelt the laughter of the children
playing in the glade,

I once heard the roundness
of a brand new tennis ball
and touched the despair of a man
with his back against the wall.

I travelled once around the world
on stars with flaming tails,
and touched the colours of my dreams
along some silver trails.

Valerie Bloom

Soft Like Bed Sheets

There is a softness in breathing,
a comfort in something I have
been doing all of my life,
that I rarely think about until
that softness is taken away.

When my chest gets tight, and air
struggles to travel past my lips;
when my nose is blocked, and air
struggles past my nostrils;
when I run for the bus, and air
feels sharp like a splinter;
these are the times that I remember
how soft breathing is.

Soft like bed sheets, soft like a cloud,
soft like the warmest hug,
like my toes on toasty green grass.

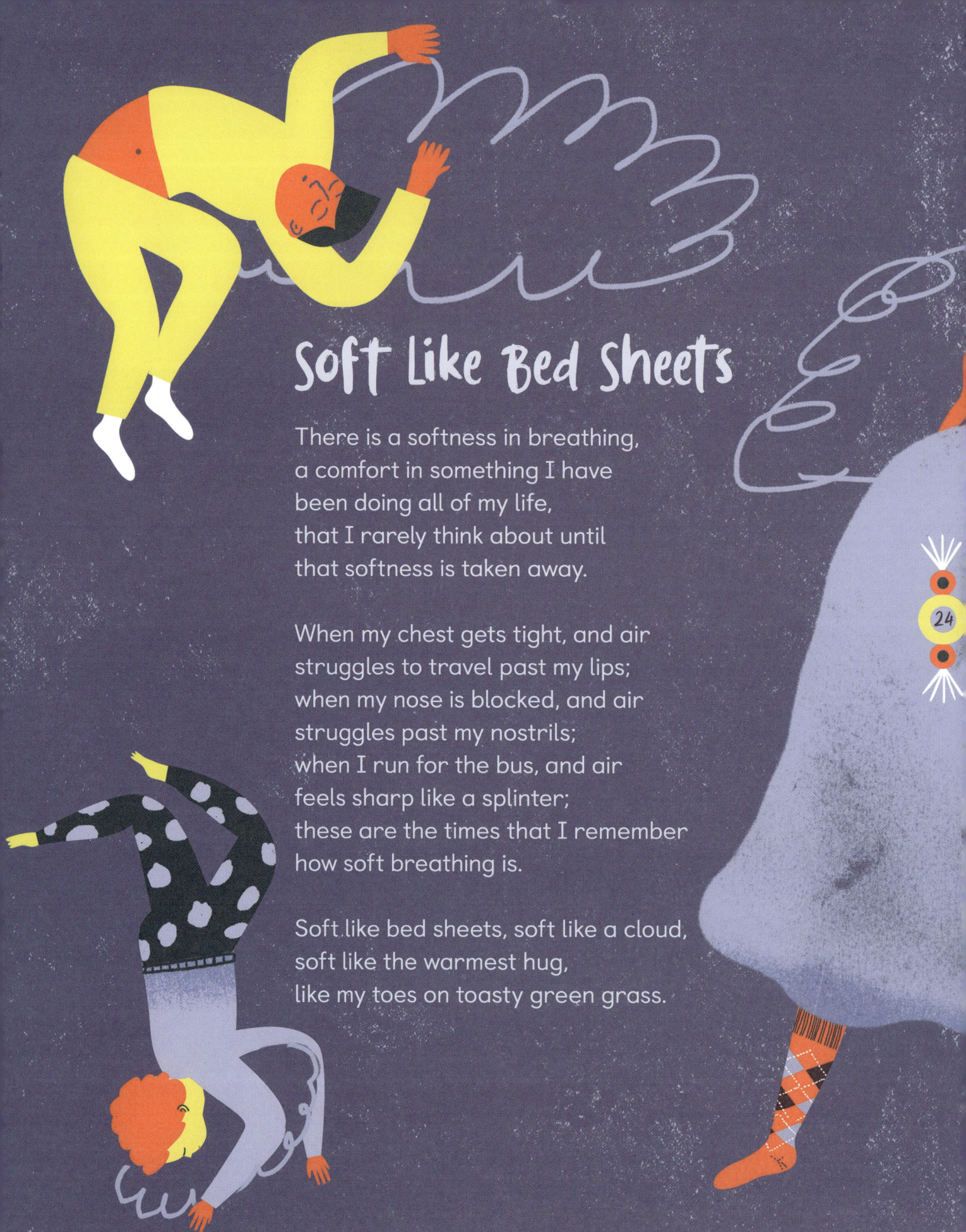

It's never nice to feel hard,
to feel sharpness and worry.
To be pushing your head above the water
when you are on dry land.
These are the moments that I remind myself
to stop and to count.

To count all of the soft things
around me and to breathe in each of them.
I breathe in my bed sheets, 1,
breathe in my pillow, 2,
breathe in the clouds, 3,
breathe in my pyjamas, 4,
breathe in the warmth from my drink, 5,
breathe in the best hug from my sister, 6,
breathe in a goodnight kiss from my mum, 7.

When the breathing is hard and the worry gets sharp,
remember to count each softness and inhale them all,
one at a time.

Amina Jama

The Rhythm of Life

Hand on the bridge
feel the rhythm of the train.

Hand on the window
feel the rhythm of the rain.

Hand on your throat
feel the rhythm of your talk.

Hand on your leg
feel the rhythm of your walk.

Hand in the sea
feel the rhythm of the tide.

Hand on your heart
feel the rhythm inside.

Hand on the rhythm
feel the rhythm of the rhyme.

Hand on your life
feel the rhythm of time
Hand on your life
feel the rhythm of time
Hand on your life
feel the rhythm of time.

Michael Rosen

Taking Care of Small Things

Today I feel tall
so big that I could
jump high above trees
leapfrog a lamppost
step on the sun's toes
catch a plane by the tail
dance up on the roof.
Today I feel tall
yet I love the small
wee, wild things that crawl
snails loving the rain
those worms on their way
I take care with my feet
tiptoe on wet paths.
And besides, who knows
maybe tomorrow
I will feel smaller
grass – impassable
the meanest anthill
seem insurmountable
but just for today
I feel strong, so tall
everything's possible
I wish that I could
somehow bottle it
to drink on small days
and when you felt that way too
I'd give some to you.

Sue Hardy-Dawson

My Inner Weather Report

Yesterday
a fierce storm
blew in
with bolts of lightning
and thunderclaps.
Pitch-black clouds
hovered overhead,
and it poured
all day long.

Today
I feel
sunny
with gentle breezes
and no clouds at all.

I'm learning
to take my inner weather report—
and notice my feelings
as they come and go.

Georgia Heard

Pausing Phases –

The seasons always simmer into clasped palms
The years fold into our past.
Everything uncontrollable revolves around us
And we try to move just as fast
Competing with stars to burn brighter
And forcing winter to callus our skin.
Obligating our whole selves to finish lines
Forgetting how beautiful things are when still.

Sophia Thakur

Anger's Secrets

the fire calls
for our attention
    don't forget to look
beneath the spark

witness the wisdom
in its crackle
it might get us
    out of the dark.

Sanah Ahsan

From *Clap When You Land*

Swimming might be the closest to flying
a human being can get. There is something
about your body displacing water

in order to propel through space that makes you feel
Godtouched. That makes me understand evolution,
that we really must have crawled up from the sea.

My life's passions
are all about water breaking, new life making,
taking breath in wrinkled flesh.

Tía tells me I am probably the daughter
of a water saint. All I know is I am most sure
of my place in the world

with the water combing my kinks,
the cold biting into my skin, & my arms
creating an arc over my head as I barrel through,

& battle too   these elements.

Elizabeth Acevedo

The Magic Box

I will put in the box

the swish of a silk sari on a summer night,
fire from the nostrils of a Chinese dragon,
the tip of a tongue touching a tooth.

I will put in the box

a snowman with a rumbling belly
a sip of the bluest water from Lake Lucerne,
a leaping spark from an electric fish.

I will put into the box

three violet wishes spoken in Gujarati,
the last joke of an ancient uncle,
and the first smile of a baby.

I will put into the box

a fifth season and a black sun,
a cowboy on a broomstick
and a witch on a white horse.

My box is fashioned from ice and gold and steel,
with stars on the lid and secrets in the corners.
Its hinges are the toe joints of dinosaurs.

I shall surf in my box
on the great high-rolling breakers of the wild Atlantic,
then wash ashore on a yellow beach
the colour of the sun.

Kit Wright

Over the Weather

We forget about the spaciousness above the clouds
but
it's up there.

The sun's up there too.

When words we hear don't fit the day,
when we worry
what we did or didn't do,
what if we close our eyes,
say any word we love
that makes us feel calm,
slip it into the atmosphere
and rise?

Creamy miles of quiet.
Giant swoop of blue.

Naomi Shihab Nye

Hide and Seek

I decided to play a game with quiet

hide and seek
my turn
I slipped into the woods
looking for quiet
instead
a cacophony of forest-crackle
a hullabaloo of beast-babble
sprang towards me while
a tweedledum of pandemonium
circled above
it was a free-for-all
and even the sun
jangled copper
between the leaves

so much for the forest

I went to the sea
searching for quiet
but the waves trumpeted
a rumbling ruckus
a crash of crinkle-crests while
squarking gulls sky-dived into
wind-trembled sea and
seashells crunched underfoot
as a medley of
fat green seaweed
slapped the sand
non-stop non-stop

so much for the sea

but then I turned
and quiet tagged me
I stopped
forest stopped
sea stopped

I found quiet
it must have been hiding
the whole time
inside my words
inside of me

Zaro Weil

Biographies

Mandy Coe

An award-winning author of eight books, Mandy Coe writes poetry for adults and children. She works in education and on literacy projects through residencies, workshops and readings.

Jack Prelutsky

Jack Prelutsky was the USA's first Children's Poet Laureate. He has filled more than fifty books of verse with his inventive wordplay, including the US bestsellers *Scranimals* and *The New Kid on the Block*. He lives in Washington State. You can visit him online at www.jackprelutsky.com.

Photo credit: Skip Kerr

Pat Mora

An award-winning author of books for children, teens and adults, Pat Mora is a literacy advocate and popular presenter. Many of her books are available in Spanish or have bilingual editions. She founded Children's Day, Book Day in 1996. CDBD is celebrated in various countries and Pat hopes it will grow further.

Kate Wakeling

Kate Wakeling grew up in Yorkshire and Birmingham. Her first collection of poems for children, *Moon Juice*, won the 2017 CLiPPA and her second collection, *Cloud Soup*, was a book of the month in the *Guardian* and *The Scotsman*.

Photo credit: Sophie Davidson

James Carter

James Carter is an award-winning children's poet and an ambassador for the UK's National Poetry Day. He has written many poetry collections, and his verse non-fiction series for Little Tiger Press has been translated into nine languages. www.jamescarterpoet.co.uk

Jason Reynolds

Jason Reynolds is a #1 *New York Times* bestselling author and winner of the 2021 CILIP Carnegie Medal. He is a Newbery Award Honoree, a Printz Award Honoree, a two-time National Book Award finalist, and was the 2020–2022 US National Ambassador for Young People's Literature. His many books include *All American Boys* and the *RUN* series.

Nikita Gill

Nikita Gill is an Irish-Indian poet who has the attention of 700,000 Instagram followers worldwide for her work. She has given a TEDx Talk, spoken at every major literary festival in the UK and been shortlisted for the Goodreads Choice Award in poetry three times. Gill has written seven poetry collections, a verse novel and a book of fables.

Joseph Coelho

The 2022–2024 Waterstones Children's Laureate, Joseph Coelho is a multi-award-winning children's author and playwright. He writes plays, picture books, non-fiction and middle grade. His recent book, *The Girl Who Became a Tree*, was shortlisted for the Carnegie Medal.

Photo credit: Hayley Madden/ The Poetry Society

Valerie Bloom

Winner of the 2022 CLiPPA, Valerie Bloom has written and edited many highly acclaimed children's poetry books; her writing is heavily influenced by her Jamaican background. She has performed widely and appeared on radio and TV. She received an MBE for services to poetry in 2007.

Amina Jama

Amina Jama is a Somali-British writer, curator, producer and facilitator. Her poetry for young people has been featured in the anthology *Rising Stars* and she has worked with CLPE on the Poetry in the Primary Classroom project.

Michael Rosen

Michael Rosen is one of Britain's best loved writers and performance poets. He has taught on MA courses in universities since 1994 and is currently Professor of Children's Literature at Goldsmiths, University of London. He was the Children's Laureate from 2007–2009 and has published over 200 books for children and adults.

Sue Hardy-Dawson

Sue Hardy-Dawson is a Yorkshire-born poet who has worked with children for 20 years. She is dyslexic and eager to encourage reluctant readers and writers. Her first solo poetry collection *Where Zebras Go* was shortlisted for the CLiPPA in 2018.

Mary Ann Hoberman

Mary Ann Hoberman was an American poet and a Children's Poet Laureate (2008–2011). She was the critically acclaimed author of over forty books for children and received an Award for Excellence in Poetry for Children, given by the National Council of Teachers of English.

Georgia Heard

Georgia Heard writes poetry for adults and children. She received her MFA in Poetry from Columbia University and has taught writing all around the world. Georgia is the founder of The Poet's Studio and the inventor of Heart Maps®. She lives with her family and dog in South Florida.

Sophia Thakur

Sophia Thakur's debut poetry collection *Somebody Give This Heart a Pen* has inspired varied audiences across the world from the Glastonbury stage to countless mainstream TV and radio segments. Her recent book *Superheroes* went straight to the bestseller list after launching.

Photo credit: Chantal Azari

Sanah Ahsan

Sanah Ahsan is an award-winning poet and a clinical psychologist, presenter, speaker and educator. Her wide-ranging work includes presenting a documentary on young people's mental health for Channel 4 and writing the poetry and lyrics for a theatre adaptation of *The Jungle Book*.

Elizabeth Acevedo

The Poetry Foundation's 2022–2024 Young People's Poet Laureate, Elizabeth Acevedo is the bestselling and award-winning author of *The Poet X* and *With the Fire on High*. She holds an MFA in Creative Writing and is a National Poetry Slam Champion. Elizabeth resides in Washington, DC.

Kit Wright

Kit Wright was born in Kent. He has worked in Canada as a lecturer, in London at The Poetry Society and was a Fellow Commoner in the Creative Arts at Trinity College, Cambridge. He lives in East London and writes for both adults and children. His latest children's collection is *The Magic Box*.

Naomi Shihab Nye

Palestinian-American poet Naomi Shihab Nye has written books for adults and children, including *Sitti's Secrets* and *Habibi*, which both won the Jane Addams Children's Book Award. She was the 2019–2022 Poetry Foundation's Young People's Poet Laureate and received the Ivan Sandrof Lifetime Achievement Award from the National Book Critics Circle in 2020.

Zaro Weil

Zaro Weil won the 2020 CLiPPA for her poetry book *Cherry Moon*. As well as a poet, she has been a dancer, theatre director, actress, playwright, educator and quilt collector to name a few. She now lives in France with a menagerie of animals.

Annalise Barber

A resident of Columbus, Ohio, Annalise Barber illustrates for children and those who are young at heart. She experiments with sinuous shapes, playful narratives and watercolour media. With a paintbrush in her hand, Annalise illustrates to inspire and empower children.

Mariana Roldán

Mariana Roldán is an illustrator based in Mexico. She loves to dance and draw. These activities are how she expresses the feelings that live inside her and how she shares with others the history of the world we live in.

Masha Manapov

Masha Manapov is an award-winning illustrator, author and image maker. Born in Baku and raised in Tel Aviv, she is currently working from her London-based studio on commissioned projects worldwide.

Nabila Adani

Nabila Adani lives in Jakarta, Indonesia, and enjoys illustrating different world cultures. She briefly worked as a product designer before moving to the United States to study children's book illustration. Now, living back in Jakarta, she enjoys illustrating and telling stories for children worldwide.

Copyright and Acknowledgements

LITTLE TIGER
An imprint of Little Tiger Press Limited
www.littletiger.co.uk
1 Coda Studios, 189 Munster Road, London SW6 6AW
Imported into the EEA by Penguin Random House Ireland,
Morrison Chambers, 32 Nassau Street, Dublin D02 YH68
First published in Great Britain 2024
P8-9, 16-17, 24-25, 30, 36-37 illustrations copyright © Masha Manapov 2024
P6-7, 14-15, 22-23, 38-39 illustrations copyright © Nabila Adani 2024
P10-11, 18-19, 28-29, 34 illustrations copyright © Annalise Barber 2024
P12-13, 20-21, 26-27, 32-33, 40-41 illustrations copyright © Mariana Roldán 2024
Cover copyright © Nabila Adani 2024
'You Are Here' from *Belonging Street* (Otter-Barry Books, 2020) by Mandy Coe © Mandy Coe 2020
Poetry selection titled: 'I Wished into a Wishing Well' from *Be Glad Your Nose Is on Your Face* by Jack Prelutsky – Illustrated by: Brandon Dorman. Text Copyright © 2008 by Jack Prelutsky. Used by permission of HarperCollins Publishers.
'My Rock' copyright © 2021 by Pat Mora. Originally published by The Poetry Foundation.
Currently published in *Poetry* Magazine. Reprinted by permission of Curtis Brown, Ltd.
'The Ink Cure' by Kate Wakeling © Kate Wakeling 2024
'How Easily' from *Weird, Wild & Wonderful* (Otter-Barry Books, 2021) by James Carter © James Carter 2021
'Your Dream Is' from *For Every One* (Knights Of, 2018) by Jason Reynolds © Jason Reynolds 2018
'A Lesson from the Trees' by Nikita Gill © Nikita Gill 2024
'Listening for Silence' by Joseph Coelho © Joseph Coelho 2024,
reproduced by kind permission of Joseph Coelho c/o Caroline Sheldon Literary Agency Ltd.
'The Colours of My Dreams' © Valerie Bloom 2021 from *Stars with Flaming Tails* (Otter-Barry Books),
reprinted by permission of Eddison Pearson Ltd on behalf of Valerie Bloom
'Soft Like Bed Sheets' by Amina Jama © Amina Jama 2024
'The Rhythm of Life' from *Michael Rosen's Big Book of Bad Things* by Michael Rosen, published by Puffin. Copyright © Michael Rosen 2010.
Reprinted by permission of Penguin Books Limited. 'The Rhythm of Life' (© Michael Rosen, 2010) is printed by permission of United Agents
(www.unitedagents.co.uk) on behalf of Michael Rosen.
'Taking Care of Small Things' from *If I Were Other Than Myself* (Troika Books, 2020)
by Sue Hardy-Dawson © Sue Hardy-Dawson 2020
'The Tree That Time Built' by Mary Ann Hoberman from *The Tree That Time Built* (Sourcebooks, 2009)
selected by Mary Ann Hoberman and Linda Winston © Mary Ann Hoberman 2009
'My Inner Weather Report' copyright © 2021 by Georgia Heard. Appears in *My Thoughts Are Clouds: Poems for Mindfulness*.
Originally published by Roaring Brook Press. Used by permission of Curtis Brown, Ltd.
'Pausing Phases –' copyright © 2019 Sophia Thakur from SOMEBODY GIVE THIS HEART A PEN by Sophia Thakur.
Reproduced by permission of Walker Books Ltd, London, SE11 5HJ www.walker.co.uk
'Anger's Secrets' by Sanah Ahsan © Sanah Ahsan 2024
Untitled poetry selection from *Clap When You Land* by Elizabeth Acevedo – Read by: Elizabeth Acevedo, Melania-Luisa
Marte. Text Copyright © 2020 by Elizabeth Acevedo. Used by permission of HarperCollins Publishers.
'The Magic Box' from *The Magic Box*, first published in 2009 by Macmillan Children's Books, an imprint of Pan Macmillan.
Reproduced by permission of Macmillan Publishers International Limited. Copyright © Kit Wright 2009
Poetry selection titled: 'Over the Weather' from *A Maze Me* by Naomi Shihab Nye – Illustrated by: Terre Maher.
Copyright © 2005 by Naomi Shihab Nye. Used by permission of HarperCollins Publishers.
'Hide and Seek' from *Cherry Moon* by Zaro Weil, copyright © 2019.
Reprinted by permission of Welbeck Children's, an imprint of Hachette Book Group, Inc.
A CIP catalogue record for this book is available from the British Library
All rights reserved • Printed in China
ISBN: 978-1-83891-564-3 • CPB/2700/2525/0823
2 4 6 8 10 9 7 5 3 1

This book includes poetry written in British and American English. Though the differences are small,
we've chosen to keep all writing in its original dialect. The messages in each poem are for everyone but
they are also rooted in the places they were dreamt up and written. We wanted to reflect this.

FSC
MIX
Paper from
responsible sources
FSC® C188448

The Forest Stewardship Council® (FSC®) is a global,
not-for-profit organisation dedicated to the promotion
of responsible forest management worldwide. FSC®
defines standards based on agreed principles for responsible
forest stewardship that are supported by environmental,
social, and economic stakeholders.

To learn more, visit www.fsc.org